A Disease

a disease called
POETRY
| MORBUS DICTUR POETICA |

Melissa M. Combs

ISBN: 978-1-962072-10-6

Cover art & design by: Melissa M. Combs

Octave
Eight
PUBLISHING
∞

octaveeightpublishing@gmail.com

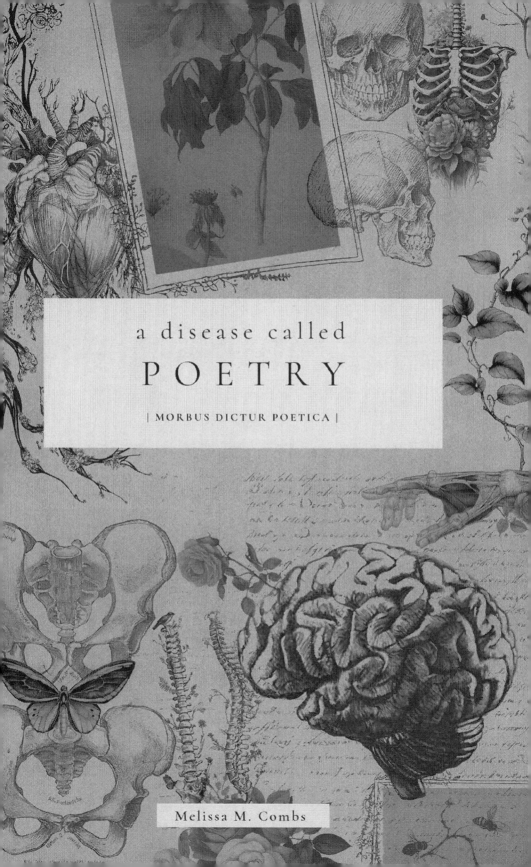

a disease called

POETRY

| MORBUS DICTUR POETICA |

Melissa M. Combs

Fig.2

SKELET

INTRODUCTION

It has long been suggested that there is a link between creativity and mental illness. Throughout time, we have witnessed major depressive disorders appear among those such as play writers, novelists, poets, and artists at a much higher rate than what we see in the general population. In the 1970's, we first heard about the link between between "madness" and "genius," (the word genius referring to literary genius, scholarly genius, and creative genius). However, speculation of such dates back at least to the time of Aristotle. In Aristotelian tradition, genius was believed to be the quality perhaps responsible for both extraordinary achievement and melancholy.

There have been many studies conducted on the correlation between mood and creativity, all resulting in varying findings. However, one thing has been agreed upon, and that is that negative emotions have been proven to increase the quantity in which a person will reflect and contemplate, ultimately leading a person to be more creative. *(Abelle, 1992; Jausovec, 1989; Kaufmann & Vosburg, 1997).*

A Disease Called Poetry is meant to act as a voice for all who suffer with any form of mental illness. For those of us that have chosen creative career paths, we are no different. Even if our emotions, or our afflictions do not always fit perfectly within the social bounds of what is deemed 'normal,' it is normal for us. May this collection make anyone (not just artists) that are suffering, in any capacity, feel seen. We are all in this together.

CAPUT UNUM | Chapter One
ANIMI | Of the Mind

CAPUT UNUM | *Chapter One*
ANIMI | *Of the Mind*

CAPUT DUO | *Chapter Two*
CORPORIS | *Of the Body*

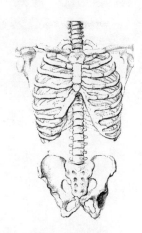

CAPUT TERIO | *Chapter Three*
CORDIS | *Of the Heart*

CAPUT TERIO | *Chapter Three*
CORDIS | *Of the Heart*

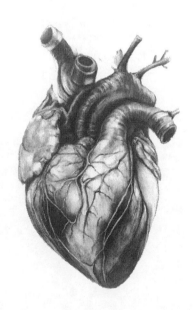

"We of the craft are all crazy. Some are affected by gaiety, others by melancholy, but all are more or less touched." – *Lord Byron*

Ad patrem gradum, qui ultim...
fratrem meum, abiisum vid...
ut postea futurum sit, vig...
annos iam lui, iterum u...
noscere. Hic denim est lex. Corpora
nostra nunquam tria sunt in...
Nostrae referat mentes nunquam
tuae marcent. Oddo quomodo ta- iam
Dum tua virtus corporalis erat, mea
spiritualis esse crevit. Hoc modo
pungunt ad momentum. Noli timere,
iustus vel... est, rituale exercitatione,

Alteri avaritia consumtus adeo...
curat, ut alios minuat;
tu autem olfacies adhuc? Anima tua
humectat. Omne mendacium quod
dicis, quem maxime amas,
die trecentos triginta tres. Pro...
frustra, in aeriali emptione, cum...
valorem perdas
in te ipso. Celeriter a genibus...
Paenitentiam quaerite, vel hoc...
infernum, non potestis relinqu...

Elapso fauces effodit avidas manus
intima mei corporis, anim et spiritus
Omnia tuleris: auferetur a vobis.
Omnia meris, tu curo tae seminabis.
Nam lux furoris est;
eadem fere, Omni silentium tu mihi
nomen obeas Mente enim iustus, ut
te prope insonis eiciam. Ac mihi
quidem innocentia, mea esse sue, m...
potentia est. Repeto. Revoca tirannis
sedendo doloris mae vivendo
paenitendo paenitendo me o...

Socrus parvi pretii me succidit, cum
iam dolor meus esset
aliter cognoscitur. Ut remediis...
valebit. Status tuos pedes tuo...
Videas te in speculo, ut clades...
cognoveris. Sic tua interiora...
exteriora, tua forma verissim...
turpis. Sit potestas tua super...
tuum, super me, pressus tua...
suffocanste. Fato conveni...
dia te quaesivi.

Offero paenitemus, mea quoque...
manu laesa. Non enim sam per...
tui similis, meditor, et vicissim...
mea vestigia redirent...
Sic hic est ad sanandum, pro nobis
qui idem volunt, et exsecrationibus
eorum quos volunt permanere,

Nocent enim, sed non potu...
intenissimos adhuc dies a...

Quem cum compuncte leger...
Omnibus tibi beneficiis, venuste re-
fundere nimirum.

Omnis enim traumatica experient
me huc adduxit; de cerebro meo re
viring.
intensam inclinationem, qua
diripienda, ac etiam nodosa, quae
neurae meatus.
restitutio erit, quae laudem ultima
... non sum complacens genus
... oculos ad quid sit quod
... profectus sum, et obtineo.
... cogitationis exempla. Novo
... tu. Limen apertum.
... versionem a me ipso pet
... delicto quod ego ipse vel
... meum commiserunt
... oportet atque implebo.
... ita leniter tracta. Dilige.
... isley.
... advocatus fidelissimus, hinc
proficiscar. Non ad perfectionem
contendo.
sed ad profectum. Hortos meo omn
tempore plantabo, carpo, plantab
Corpus meum iubebo movere, ut e
... nos et annos convictis expellere
... no plus nimio tabescere.
... mature. Habeo semina ad
... dum et amandum ut cresca
... llorum sum, satis scio.
... orpus, inquam, et sic est.
... im secans, et superficies.
... hoc cor perculit.
... magis eam sanare credo
... humanum vis est
... Aperta invitatio ad dolor
... iam incubator sanationis.
... superbus sum de me ipso,
... fido in processu, ad vindicand
meum palum.
novorum initiis hereditas. Nolo e
diu lupam Renati.
Saltare choros, cantate canticum.
paradoxa esse significatum est per
omnia.

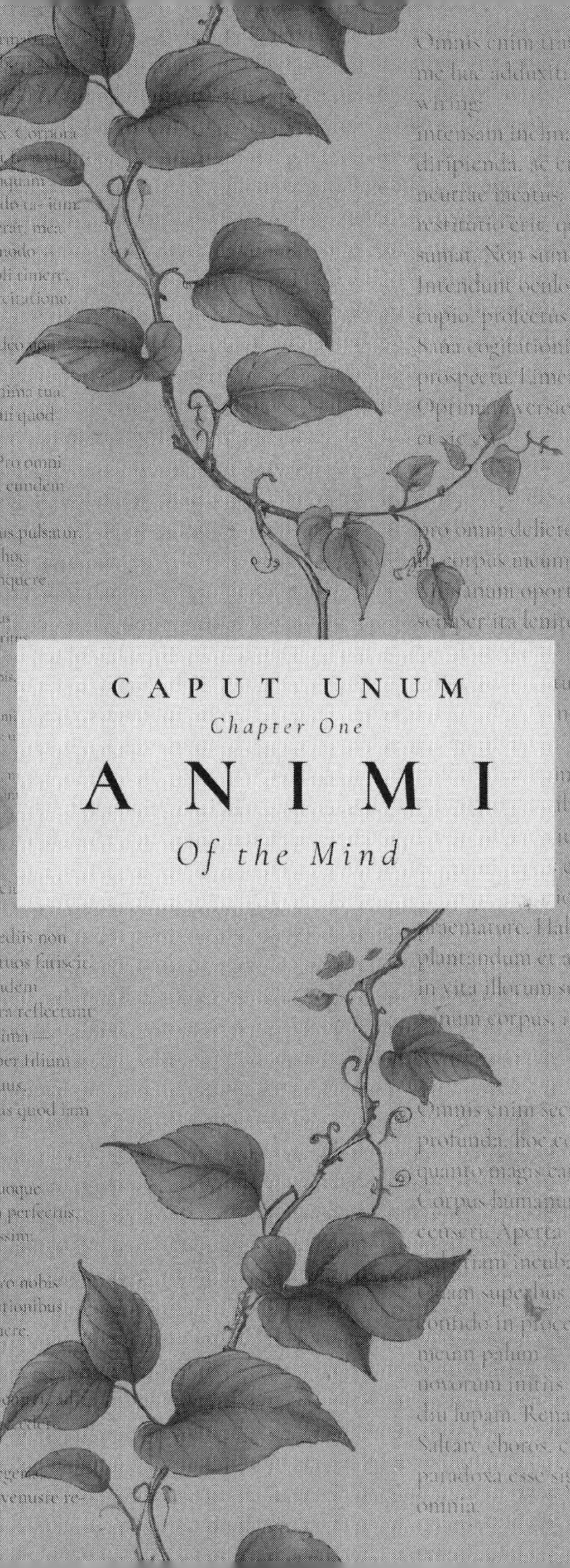

CAPUT UNUM

Chapter One

ANIMI

Of the Mind

These jumbled thoughts —
pretty mysteries and petty miseries,
some may call it poetry.
For me, it feels more like an infirmity.
Where something,
or someone is gripping me at the seams,
ripping me wide open, until I scream.
My thoughts and aching heart
spewing out, uncontrollably.

Poetry, they call it.
I call it a disease.

I don't hate my depression
as much as I hate having to bottle it all in.
I hate this stupid lipstick,
and this smile I've learned to fake.
This fraudulent side of me.
I hate my ability to act.
Your average human being,
but I deserve some sort of grammy.
I hate that my laugh is convincing.
And that with a face full of makeup,
I'm cat called, and told that I am pretty.
Everyone passes by me.
I blend in.
No one seems to be worried.
So no, I don't hate my depression.
I hate living in a world where
no one really knows me.

One day everyone I love is going to die.

What new plant should I add to my collection,
Pothos or Bonsai?

I live in a world where poverty, murder,
and world hunger still exists.

Those photos I took at the art festival,
I should definitely make prints.

There's a cure for cancer,
but they won't tell us what it is.

Colorodo, or California, for vacation this year?

(Funny how us humans fixate on the
meaningless to avoid the thoughts we all fear.)

It's a lucid dream.
It's a made up thing.
It's anything and everything
I decide it to be.

Life —
my thoughts
are what give it all meaning.
I just can't ever seem to control them.
I dig into my brain
to unscramble, and organize,
only for my hands to come up bloody;
my memories bleeding out,
dripping into the lives of others around me.
I swear I don't mean to be so messy;
to eject all this negativity, uncontrollably.

Then again, why do I care?
It's a lucid dream. It's a made up thing.

I'm hollow to the touch.
You could stick your hands right through me,
and I can assure you, there is nothing left to pull out.
I'm a ghost of who I once was.

You can see it in my eyes most days.
You can hear it in my voice.

I wish it were different.
But sometimes trauma doesn't leave us a choice.

I'm not a fan of calling it quits.
I stay until my faith looks stupid.
I strive until my body grows weak.
I recite affirmations until my tongue
renders itself useless and I can't speak.
I believe in love long after it dies,
and well into some fictional after-life.
I am an artist,
delusional and tortured; diseased.

They told me to stand out,
and to avoid fitting in,
as if it were something
I would one day be proud of.
Only problem now,
where do I go to hide,
when standing out feels
a little too brave?

You ask me to bring you into my world,
but I'm lost inside of my own mind.
No sense of direction.
No sense of time.

If it were a map,
it would be filled with nameless countries
and empty guides.
And the most impressive spot
I could take you, would be a stop sign.

We'd stop and get stuck
on the corner of Fear Drive and Anxiety Street.

Then next thing you know,
you're lost inside of this unimpressive world,
right there beside me.

Do yourself a favor,
keep roaming.
Stay free.

You wouldn't know it,
but my logic is a siren, sounding first.

My emotions just happen
to be good at skipping line.

The problem with me is,
I'll tell you until I'm blue the face just
how much I don't need you —
or anyone, at that.

But that's not true.
It's just that everyone I've ever needed
turned out not to need me.

I guess I just think it's safer now
for me to be the first one to leave.

I go from wanting to be liked,
to giving a shit less.

Somedays others pull the strings,
and I am the puppet,
foolishly; willingly.

And other days,
I gather the courage to tell
those deserving of it to fuck off.

I'm unapologetically both versions of me.
Split in the dead center of my personality.

I was a couple bucks below the line of poverty,
and just a few wires short of finding my sanity.

And that's the story of how wine became my therapy.

As a child
they want to label you
almost as soon as you exit the womb.
And if not then,
at least by the time you make it into high school.

Bipolar, ADHD, depression, split personality.
Because for the world surrounding you
there is no accountability.

You lived through divorce,
you witnessed death,
you were sexually assaulted.
But it's never the world,
it's always you, the child, that is faulted.

What a fucked up system.
What an injustice to us, as children.
When is enough, enough?
When will they stop popping the tops off of
prescription pills?
When will they stop labeling us?

We were never broken.
The world was.

"You aren't thin enough, you look like a cow."
Five months of bulimia |
"What about now?"

"God you're so vain."
Starts reading ancient text, and seeking depth |
 "Can I pray for you?"

"Lol, you're so lame."
Picks up two hobbies, and learns a new trade |
"Hey, look!"

"Ew, what a show off! You're not even that great."

(It's tough being human in a world filled with jealousy and hate.)

If I keep quiet,
my demons wrap their pointed,
infected nails tightly around my throat,
choking me — my very essence escaping me.

If speak my mind though,
I perform my own exorcism, you see.

My tongue, unfiltered; my mind, set free.

Sometimes my heart beats so fast
I swear my chest is getting ready to uncage it.
My mind races, as if it's running on an outdated
operating system, unequipped to process
necessary downloads.
My body shakes, and my knees buckle.
Twenty pounds of bone,
making a mockery of its own existence.

But, "that's okay," my Dr. says,
"there are pills for that."

In other words, I'm sick and I'm broken.
But, with the right structure of molecules,
he can mask that.

Are they trust issues,
or did I observe
and store away the
repeated patterns
of deception and betrayal
and form my own internal
protection system?

When I lock you out
and throw away the key,
am I being cynical,
or am I guarding all that
I truly have? *Me*.

My thoughts teleport me to a time
when you were mine.
My words comfort me to a point of
believing my illusive storyline.
Reality flees me.

As a child I was taught to speak
only when spoken to.
Sit up straight.
Say, "yes ma'am," and "yes sir."
Don't you know it's rude to stare?
Cross your t's and dot your i's.
"Please" and "thank you."
Move over and let the elders by.
Stop your crying.
Quit your whining.
Hold still while you get your striking.
Do as your told,
don't question what I say.
There's too much work to do,
how dare you ask to play!

I was told I was learning manners,
but all it seems I really learned was to
fall in line,
in a world that preys on those
without spines.

I hate myself for the smallest things.
Like stepping on a spider, unintentionally.
Buying my children blue water bottles,
when they asked for green.
Being treated like shit by someone,
and in response, losing my composure,
and in turn, being mean.

Yet I forgive others for nearly everything.
My stupid, foolish, weak, empathy.
For others, I mean.
Cause I never seem to leave any for me.

Divorce.
It's never a child's fault.
But what's tragic,
is they, products of both parents,
absorb both of their pain.
It's not their fault,
but they sure do feel that way.

This world is loud.
My thoughts, even louder.
For an over-thinker,
there is no where to run and hide.
Not from the world.
And especially not from myself.

You created me,
the villain.
Don't go playing
hero now.

You don't get to
"save me"
from the destruction
you set before me.

Societal norms are a bore.
I prefer an on your toes,
hair on end,
skin crawling,
gut reaction.

In other words,
let me be your
deviant,
unorthodox distraction.

A tangled mind.
A tainted heart.
A troubled soul.
A terrifying human-being.

I have a problem with wanting to leave before being left.
My therapist tells me that it is unhealthy.
And I must agree.

But I dare someone tell that to the younger me.
The me who stayed through absolutely everything,
the me — used and betrayed,
the me — cheated on and rejected,
beaten down, and dejected.

And while I wish to one day learn how to trust again;
how to stay...
I give myself grace, right now, for being this way.

You cross my mind from time to time.
Yes, even still.
Even though I've finally healed.

You don't seem to linger the way you
did before though.
It's quick. It's blurry.
If I didn't know any better,
I'd say my mind is in a hurry.

I mean, who can blame it?
You once hijacked my every thought,
and embedded yourself deep into
it's tissue.
It was problematic,
the way I would obsessively miss you.

You — you were quite the issue.

I like where I'm at now though.
Clear neural pathways.
Logic transmitting signals
to all regions of my brain.

When you enter in now,
you're treated as an intruder.

You're allowed just long enough for me
to remember something trivial,
like your stupid, gorgeous face...
and sometimes, the memory of
the way you'd say my name.

Then you're gone again.
And I happen to prefer it this way.

Time –
it's healing, they say.

Yeah,
but it also drags
the memory of you
further away.

Being a kid sucks.
You're punished for your family's sins,
judged by their dividends.
Mocked for the only shoes
your family could afford.

Think that's bad?
Wait! There's more!

Your value is directly tied to the clothes
you wear, and the car you drive.
You're expected to make all A's,
and join all clubs, but you're hiding in
the bathroom, terrified.
Your grades begin to drop,
and your parents get mad.
Little do they know,
you're just trying to survive.

Being a kid should be easier, right?
After all, you're still young.
Still so new to this thing called life.

None of us are holy.
We're just hypocrites,
making the same mistakes,
in different seasons,
and in different ways.

I think by the time our hands
are clean,
amnesia sneaks up,
and we pretend we've lived
our lives so perfectly.

So we cast our stones,
and we do more damage.
All the while,
forgetting
we too, have many times,
mismanaged.

What if I treated you like the trash that you treat me?
Tied you up until you feel so worthless you can't breathe?
What if I filled you day in and day out, 13 gallons of words
that had no business living, but were meant only to be
wasted?

What if I, though I claimed to love you,
made you feel absolutely abandoned;
left for dead and implicitly hated?

Would you still want my hands to be
the last hands that held you?

Well,
these hands no longer wish to.
Even as trash.
Let someone new take you out.

Last night, I was crying in my shower
with a bottle of wine.
Today, my god complex resurfaced.
I'm more than fucking fine.

Tell me there is a hell that exists,
or I can assure I will not rest in peace.

Tell me it's burning sulfur,
helpless screams, and in vain pleas.

Tell me there is a place where the
monsters all bleed out.
A heavenly paradox
where my vengeance may feed,
and justice is brought about, finally.
Where the rapists, the pedophiles,
and the murderers are tortured indefinitely.

Somewhere where I may
carry out my righteous anger,
without mercy; ever so passionately.
Tell me, or I will not rest in peace.

From my tomb,
I will curse and chant spells
until I myself have awakened the
bodies and bones of all the innocent;
until we unite together ourselves to
create this hell.

People don't just *snap*.
There's a shift that occurs.
A signaling malfunction.
It's scientifically proven,
and it can, in fact, be mapped.
Then after the mapping,
they'll begin rewiring,
and you'll begin healing.

By the way, that's good
news for the rich
and shit news for the poor.
Because, there's a price tag on us all,
telling medical staff who to care for more,
or at all, actually.

So, I hope you were born to the right ethnicity,
and your family's pockets are filled with lump sums
of money. Because, whether you like it or not,
this world is built on partiality.

And now that you know that health isn't free,
best of luck to you, on your quest to re-attain your
mental health, and your sanity.

I have a big heart and a tiny backbone.
I have no problem loving others,
but I can never find it in myself to love me.
I think I'm sick.
I think I was born with some kind of
deformity.

At this point, it's painfully comical.
They tell me to "relax, just be."

Meanwhile, I'm thinking about thinking,
over-stimulated,
and obsessing...
over every nanoscopic spec floating
around me.
Over every gesture made.
Every word.
Every glance.
Every little, insignificant thing.

Someone please tell those that are healthy,
you can't "just be," when you live with
chronic anxiety.

It's beautiful outside.
What? You can't see it; touch it; smell it?

Something prohibiting you from feeling it inside?
Silly girl, you thought love would keep you alive?

I know it's convincing,
but that's not the sun in the sky.
That's metal and Ammonium nitrate.
No other choice but to believe,
as sixty percent of your body's water evaporates.
Still you love it.
Reach both hands to the sky to touch it.

Dehydrate.
Detonate.

Pay close attention as your balance abandons you.
You worship what is too bright.
Tones not meant for the consumption of the human eye.
You bow to it's beams.
You're desperate for it's hue.
All along, it sets out to annihilate you.

Ad patrem gradum, qui affirmat
fratrem meum abusum vidi,
ut postea futurum sit, vigilavero
annos tam fui, iterum co...
noscere. Hic donum est. Lex. Corpora
nostra numquam tam sunt ut...
Nostrae tenerae mentes numquam
tuae marcent. Oddo quomodo ta... tum.
Dum tua virtus corporalis erat, mea
spiritualis esse crevit. Hoc modo
pungam ad momentum. Noli timere.
Iustus vel verit. rituale exercitatione.

Alteri avaritia consumpsit adeo ut...
erat, ut alios minuat;
tu autem olfacies adhuc? Anima tua,
humectat. Omne mendacium quod
dicis, quem maxime amas,
die trecentos triginta tres. Pro omni
frustra. materiali emptione, eundem
valorem perdas
in te ipso. Celeriter a genibus pulsatur.
Paenitentiam quaerere, vel hoc...
infernum, non potestis relinquere.

Elapso luces effodit avidas tonus
intima mei corporis, animi et spiritus.
Omnia talem; auferetur a vobis.
Omnia meris, tu quoque semibibus.
Nam lux furata est;
eodem feres. Omne silentium tu mihi
nomen obeas. Mente enim lusisti ut
te prope manus eleceris. Ac mihi
quidem innocentia, mea essem; mea
potentia est. Repetam. Revoca tuum onus
sedendo doloris mei vivendo
picticando picticando me su...

Socrus parvi pretii me succidit, cum
iam dolor meus esset
aliter cognoscitur. Ut remediis non
valebit. Status tuos pedes tuos fatiscit.
Videas te in speculo, ut eadem
cognoveris. Sit tua interiora reflectunt
exteriora; tua forma verissima —
turpis. Sit potestas tua super filium
tuum, super me, pressus tuus,
suffocans te. Fato conventus quod iam
diu te quaesivi.

Offero paenitemus, mea quoque
manu laesa. Non enim sum perfectus,
tui similis, meditor. et vicissim,
mea vestigia redire.
Sic hic est ad sanandum, pro nobis
qui idem volunt. et exsecrationibus
eorum quos volunt permanere.

Nocent enim, sed non poena ad
intensissimos adhuc dies...

Quem cum compuncte legere...
Omnibus tibi beneficiis, venuste re-
fundere nimirum.

Omnis enim traumatica experient
me huc adduxit, de cerebro meo re
wiring:
intensam inclinationem, qua
diripienda, ac etiam nodosa, quae
neutrae meatus;
restitutio erit, quae laudem ultima
sumat. Non sum complacens genus.
Intendunt oculos ad quid sit quod
cupio, profectus sum. et obtineo.
Sana cogitationis exempla. Novo
prospectu. Limen apertum.
Optimam aversionem a me ipso pet

quod ego ipse vel
...mmiserunt
...atque implebo,
...tracta. Dilige.

...fidelissimus. hinc
...ni ad perfectionem

...rofectum. Hortos meo om
...plantabo. carpo. plantabo
...meum iubebo movere. ut e
...et annos convictis expellere
...plus nimio tabescere.
...ture. Habeo semina ad
...ndum et amandum ut cresca
...illorum sum. satis scio.
...o corpus, inquam; et sic est

...enim secans. et superficies.
...hoc cor pertulit.
...magis eam sanare credo
...mamanam vis est
...Aperta invitatio ad dolore
...am incubator sanationis.
...um superbus sum de me ipso.
...onfido in processu. ad vindicandi
meum palum
novorum initiis hereditas. Nolo e
diu lupam. Renati.'
Saltare choros. cantate canticum V
paradoxa esse significatum est per
omnia.

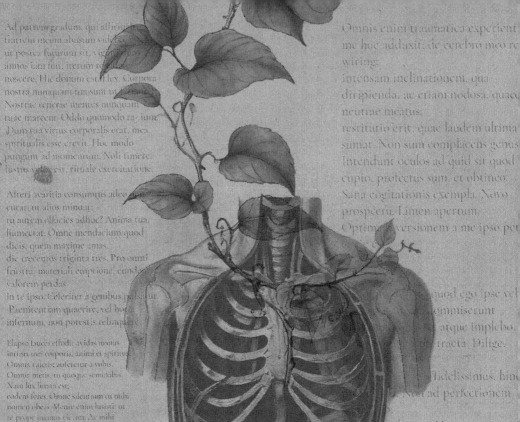

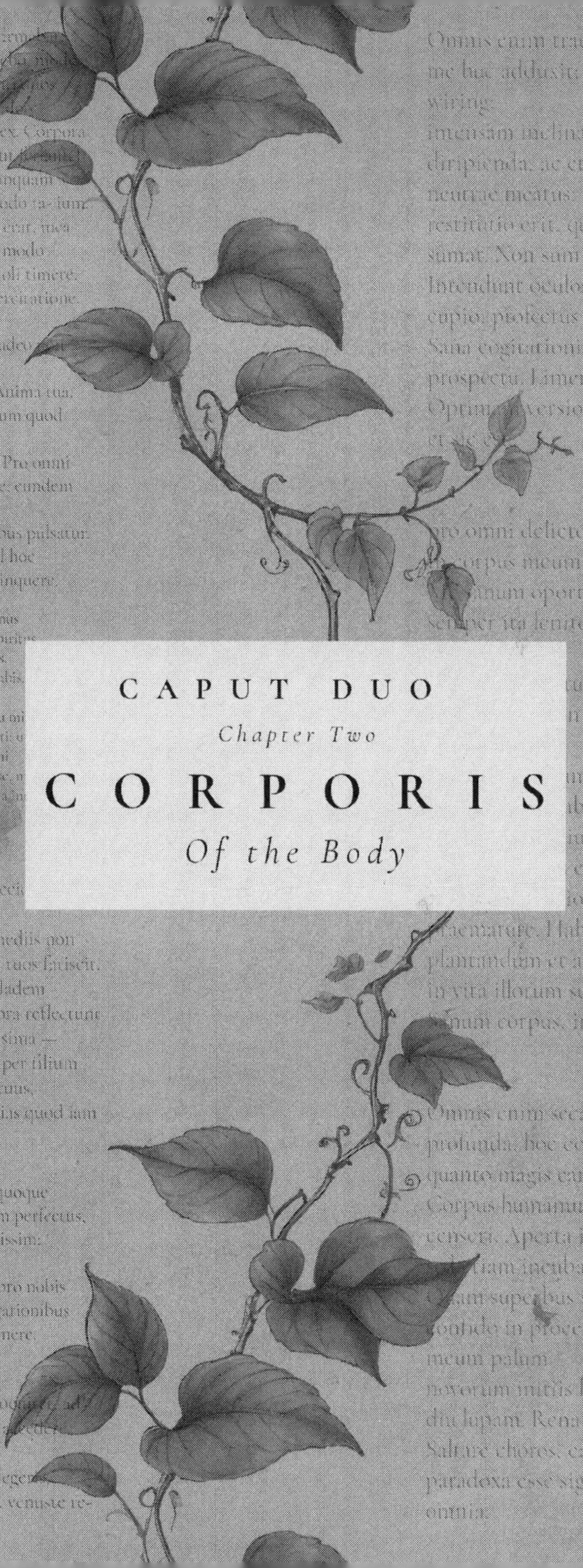

CAPUT DUO

Chapter Two

CORPORIS

Of the Body

God damn it, I did it again.
I'm losing weight,
but more than likely at the
expense of my teeth.
Was it worth it to watch
my stomach bloat leave,
just to watch my gums bleed?

I wonder if anyone heard me.
Was I too loud?
Will they notice my smeared
lipstick? Did I take too long
in there? Will they be worried?

*"Have you lost weight, dear?
You're glowing. You're so pretty."*

Wow. Not the reaction I was
expecting. Not the reaction I'm
even sure I needed.
Those compliments —
this disorder —
it's that right there.
That's what feeds it.

Every compliment evades me.

I'm still the girl with the gap in her teeth.
Still the chubby girl that the boys all teased.
I'm still seven year old, ugly duckling, me.

You weren't my real parent,
but I looked to you all the same.
And yet, all I ever found was your hatred for me,
that unfortunately transformed into my own shame.
Your real daughter was the only one
that seemed to live up to the standards of
your family's name.
Embarrassed to introduce me to your colleagues
or friends, I picked up on that,
at the young age of ten.
Subtle expressions,
and disgusted glances.
I learned what your stance was.
I learned the importance of blood and genetics.
So, why, when you were the one that shunned me,
was I the one so apologetic?
I chased your love, and was met instead with a fist,
hands around my throat, and your thumbprints
digging into my wrists.
You crucified me, you know?
Gave me a cross to bear.
Unconcealed markings that I still to this day,
wish would not show.
To be your step-child was to ask to be loved,
and to be told no.
And I can't pretend that to this day,
the trauma from that does not follow.

We're born into a world,
kicking, screaming, crying.
Why?
If I had to guess,
it's because from the moment
we take our very first breath,
the clock then starts,
and we're slowly dying.
As babies,
we don't know this yet.
But I think inside of us there's a siren
signaling, something's just not right.

I thought being thin and beautiful
as a little girl was an honor.
My mother always told me my
beauty was the topic amongst
the moon and the stars.
But at the young age of nine,
his hands left scars.
And by the time he was finished
with me,
all I can tell you,
is I've spent the remainder
of my life cursing the moon
and rebuking those stars.

I have allowed cold hands to caress my cheeks,
arms that felt more like cages, than protection,
to ensure a "safe keep."
I have taken in the voices of manipulation,
sounding like love, but designed to keep me weak.
I have given away my innocence, vulnerability, and
dignity to far too many that were unworthy.

Now it's time I advocate for me.

A part of me
I lost that day,
when I allowed
you back into my life;
when I handed over,
once more,
my body.
I guess feeling
your touch again
was worth more than
my dignity.

Doing everything I can to feel alive.
Morning breaks dawn,
bringing light to last night's regrets.
I capsize.
I'm drowning in an ocean of lies.
That wasn't love.
Those were the hands of a devil,
gripping my thighs.

Us tangled in your sheets was a false religion.
You were the cult leader, and I was your
innocent church girl, hands reaching to the sky,
seeking redemption —
redemption that I never did find.

You called it blind faith.
I now know I was just *blind*.

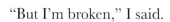

"But I'm broken," I said.

"That's okay. I'm broken too. Undress, and let me inside of you."

I didn't know where or to whom to turn,
when loving him made a sinner of me.
My lust for him stained my purity,
and my stubborn dedication
bent and broke my wings.
I was damned,
and no one but him, could save me.

There are too many young girls
scrubbing violently at their
bodies — not to get clean,
but to wash the shame away.
Shame that was never theirs
to intake.
Their bodies,
encompassing their very essence;
bright, talented, beautiful souls,
treated as something only physical.
Selfish men stealing all control.

They say women like me
are bratty and unruly.
Aggressive and violent.
Too much for this world.
A lost cause,
nothing will help,
not even a psychiatrist.

Bet they would be labeled too,
if at the young age of ten,
they were physically abused.
But, holier than thou,
that's the role they choose.

I did what I could to survive.
Taught myself to toughen up.
I just wanted a fair chance at life.

When I was just a young girl,
before I heard the voices telling me,
"you're too big for that swimsuit," or, "you're not built right
for a two-piece," I just simply loved the way the water from
the sea felt like nourishment to my soul. Every grain of sand
was magic beneath my feet. How could my steps cause
indentions, yet I did not sink? There was no time to consider
myself, and such fleeting insignificance, as skin-deep beauty.
I was in love with this great big world, faithfully surrounding
me. A bathing suit was not a statement piece. I simply put it
on as a necessity, so that I may drench my skin in sun, and
heal from the salt of the sea.

Why did the voices of the world, at the age of seven,
choose to be so unkind to me?
Ugly, fat, awkward, chubby.
Those voices have spoken, their words fall dead, and yet the
echo still, quite often, floats around in my head.

Child-like wonder dissipates,
and the poisoned seeds have taken root inside of me.

As a child, I just wanted to be free.
Just wanted to live. Wanted to be.
Why did no one notice or advocate for me?

Pretty privilege, they call it.
But it is no privilege to enter rooms
greeted with death glares,
or to be spoken down to, with envy,
instead of being spoken to with empathy.

You're hated before you're even known.
Written off before being introduced.
As if they're scared their man may be seduced,
and their own appeal reduced.

You try your best to be seen for your kindness,
determination, your actions; your heart.

But your "pretty privilege" obscures
their view before you can so much as start.

I've never worshipped the devil,
but I once knelt to a man, standing 6'2.
I've never practiced witchcraft,
but I whispered obscenities into his ears,
just to watch him come unglued.
I've never pinned a voodoo doll,
but I dug my nails into different parts
of his body, with intentions set in mind —
first, his heart, just below his belt line,
and lastly, his spine.

I've never cast a circle,
or chanted an ancient spell.
Unless you count this poem,

and he fell,
      and he fell,
            and he fell.

You think you
took and used my body,
but I made an alter of your bed,
and a mess of your head.

My curves cursed you.
My skin tainted you.
My tongue, to this day,
is a weapon, and my words
destroy you.

My daddy issues shouldn't be sexy.
Stop capitalizing off my trauma.
The lack of love I received is not
an open permission entry for you
to slide into intimate parts of me.
I was a child who deserved more.
Now I'm an adult advocating
that I receive.
And *no,*
you cannot be my new "daddy."

I'd rather be Lilith, than Eve.
Rather be deemed the harlot,
than a blissful, ignorant, housewife.
I'd rather promise futures to men
just to rob them of them,
than be cheated on, not just once,
but twice, and thereon after,
for the remainder of my life.

I'd rather be the one calling the shots,
and sharpening the knives.

Bending the rules,
and breaking hearts.
Loving myself more
than I love playing their meaningless parts.

He was a playboy.
He used my body,
and I counted down the
seconds until he spilled out,
deeming himself "free."

But I was a poet,
I had to teach him...
not a commodity.
For every meaningless thrust,
and shallow stare,
I stroked pen to paper,
cursing him to find me
everywhere.

Now even when
he lies with what is soft,
healing, and kind,
I am the dark seduction he cannot
bear to leave behind.

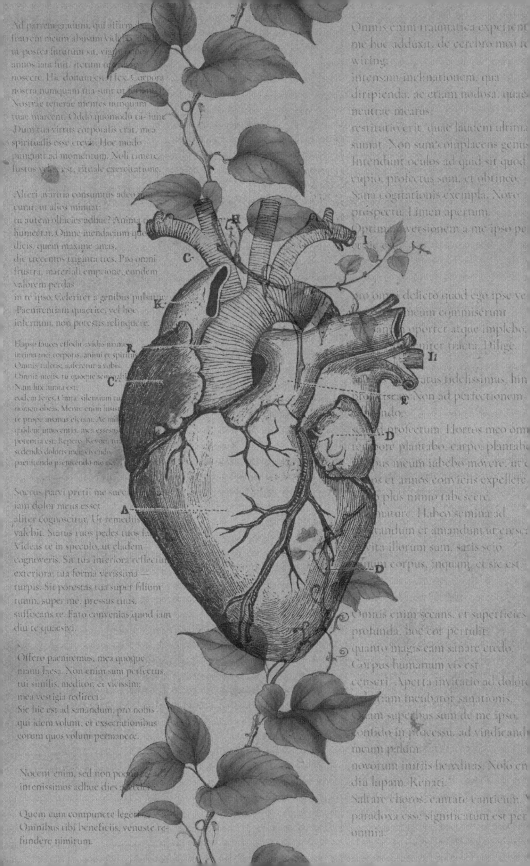

Ad parvi negotium, qui affirm...
fratrem meum abusum valeris...
ut postea saturum sit, vig...
annos iam fuit, iterum...
noscere. Hic donum est ut... Corpora
nostra numquam tua sunt ut...
Nostrae tenerae mentes numquam
tuae marcent. Odi, quomodo tu... sunt
Dum tua virtus corporalis erat, mea
spiritualis esse crevit. Hoc modo
pungunt ad monitum. Noli timere,
iustus ut... est, rituale exercitatione.

Alteri avaritia consumptus adeo non
curat, ut alios minuat;
tu autem officies adhuc? Anima...
humectat. Omne mendacium quo...
dicis, quam maxime amas,
die trecentos triginta tres. Pro omni
frustra, materiali emptione, eundem
valorem perdas
in te ipso. Celeriter a genibus pulsatur.
Paenitentiam quaerite, vel hoc
infernum, non potestis relinquere.

Elapso faces effodit avidis manu...
interna mei corporis, animi et spiritu...
Omnis talcris; auferetur a nobis.
Omnia meis, tu quoque se... plu...
Nam lux aurata est;
eodem feres. Omne silentium tu...
nomen obeis. Mente enim iussi...
te prope insanus eiciam. Ac nihil...
eiusdem innocentia, mea essent...
potentia est. Reperio. Revoco. ...
sedendo doloris mei, ex credo...
paenitendo paenitendo me se...

Socrus parvi pretii me suce...
iam dolor meus esset
aliter cognoscitur. Ut remediis...
valebit. Status tuos pedes tuos l...
Videas te in speculo, ut eadem
cognoveris. Sic tua interiora reflectu...
exteriora; tua forma verissima —
turpis. Sic potestas tua super filium
tuum, super me, pressas tuas,
suffocans te. Fato convenias quod iam
diu te quaesivi.

Offero paenitemus, mea quoque
manu laesa. Non enim sum perfectus,
tui similis, meditor; et vicissim;
mea vestigia redirect
Sic hic est ad sanandum, pro nobis
qui idem volunt, et exsecrationibus
eorum quos volunt permanere.

Nocent enim, sed non poss...
interissimos adhuc dies a...

Quem cum compuncte leger...
Omnibus tibi beneficiis, venuste re-
fundere nimirum.

Omnis enim traumatica experient...
me huc adduxit; de cerebro meo r...
ut ring.
intensam inclinationem, qua
diripienda, ac etiam nodosa, quae...
neutrae meae us...
restitutio erit, quae laudem ultima...
sumat. Non sum complacens genus
Intendunt oculos ad quid sit quod
cupio, profectus sum, et obtineo.
Sana cogitationis exempla. Novo
prospectu. Limen apertum.
Optimam aversionem a me ipso pe...
...

...ro ipso, delicto quod ego ipse ve...
...meum commiserunt
...oportet atque implebo,
...iter tracta. Dilige
...atus fidelissimus, hin...
...nse... Non ad perfectionem...
...nado;
...secum profectum. Hortos meo om...
...tempore plantabo; carpo; plantab...
...us meum iubebo movere, ut...
...os et annos conviciis expellere
...plus nimio tabescere.
...mature. Habeo semina ad
...andum et amandum; ut cresc...
...vita illorum sum, satis scio.
...m corpus, inquam, et sic est.

Omnis enim secans, et superficies
profunda, hoc est pertulit;
quanto magis eam sanare credo.
Corpus humanum vis est
censeri. Aperta invitatio ad dolore...
...am incubator sanationis
...um superbus sum de me ipso,
...confido in processu, ad vindicand...
meum pritiu...
novorum initiis hereditas. Nolo en...
dia lupam. Renati.
Saltare choros, cantate canticum,
paradoxa esse significatum est per...
omnia.

CAPUT TERIO

Chapter Three

CORDIS

Of the Heart

I've endured wild fires
in this body.
Not the kind you see in
California.
But I can tell you,
the rage and fury of those are
of similar magnitude.

I yearn for a water to put me out,
still I burn for *you*.

3am,
the witching hour.

We lied awake just talking.
Laughter filled the room.
I let my guard down,
and in, I invited you.

A moment seemingly natural,
I learned that night was supernatural.

3am,
I fell in love, and under your spell.

Go ahead, love her,
to atone your undying hatred for me.
Hold her every night,
ever so tightly, as you squeeze out
what little life you've left inside of me.
Kiss her until your lips are finally
rid of my name.
Pin her to the bed
and gently claim her,
as I disown my own self
with the utmost disgust.

I guess I only have myself to blame,
for believing in us.

By now we should all
be tired of comparing battle scars.

We're all wounded, okay?

At the end of it all,
every one of us was born
into a world where every day
is nothing more than playing
Russian roulette.
Intrusive thoughts of
what comes next.
Will the bullet miss me,
or will today be the day I
fall to my death?

To be human is to be harmed.

So lets stop making life harder.
We can make the choice to *disarm*.

You called me weak for loving you,
so I became strong.
I learned to pity you instead.

For what kind of man
leads on the one who loves him
to his very core,
down dark and barren paths
until she is no more?

You tell her all these awful things about me.

I get it, *I guess.*

If I were her,
and she knew how much I loved and fought for you,
I'd die too.
If she felt both the weight and gravity of the way
you would let go of, only to chase after me —
the push and pull,
the ebb and flow,
the resemblance of our love and the law of the universe.
(Everything this world was founded on,
everything that we know.)
It's too much.
We were too much.
You called me your *destiny.*

I get it now.
It's best she believes these awful things about me.

I'm afraid to be that happy ever again,
because I still remember the crash-land.

Being high is fun, until you fall down.

When flying, you feel weightless;
you feel free.
Until you hit the ground.
Until you bloody your knees.

Loving you was harmless, until it wasn't.
Until you stopped loving me.

It wasn't that I hated the ring.
It's that the one I loved,
versus the one you bought me,
was exactly the same price.
You asked me which one I'd prefer,
and I told you, *twice.*

See, it's not that I hated the ring,
I hated that it felt as if you were
never listening.

With recurrent thoughts of her,
how could you ever stop to consider me?

I didn't hate the ring.
I hated being second choice.
I hated *Katie.*

I've been high without the weed.
Drunk without the booze.
Been up in the clouds, stone cold sober.
I've been so confused.

This world just doesn't make sense,
after losing you.

You called me up, in the middle of a break down.
And in the eye of your hurricane,
I found peace.

Isn't this the way connection works?
The sum of the equation being
your brokenness + mine = wholeness?

I've never been good at math.
I see numbers and it's all a blur.
But loving you, and each and every one of your demons,
that I could see myself being good at.
Words, I've been told I'm good at those.
I could be the one each night,
lying my head on your chest,
whispering into your ear,
poetry and prose.

With my finger, ever so gently,
I could trace you personalized love letters over
the most intimate parts of your skin.
I could love you the way a poet loves.

You just have to let me in.

I don't even get to keep my dignity enough to say
that I was your second choice. I wasn't next in line.
I was just *in* line. I don't even know that I was there
because of any of my qualities,
(unless lack of love for myself and desperation count).
My only question is... when you saw the way that
I loved you, why not kick me out? I would have rather
lost my place in line, than wasted all of these years
(to be exact, five).
I loved you as if it was some sort of prerequisite;
something that would bring us both back to life.
You used me though. Filled me with lies, and in turn,
ripped away at pieces of my soul. As if from the start,
I was ever even whole. You left me empty. Sent me
scavenging the floor for your love. Ooh, look!
Another bread crumb; another tiny piece.
I picked them all up, one by one, in hopes of gathering
enough to finally eat.

But you were never going to be my seven course meal,
much less, any kind of meal for me.
I was always going to be hungry for your love.
In fact, I was always going to be left starving.

Careful who you let lead you.
Some lead with love, like a church.
Others lead with lies, like a cult.

I'll never forget the day you called me
a "weak woman."
Truthfully, because I was.
At any given moment, liable to give way
and shatter under the pressure of it all.

The weight of losing you, too heavy.
The task of moving on, too tall.

You could command it.
I would open my arms,
and I would trust fall.
My faith in you was child-like,
and my love for you was blind.
You could sin against me,
and I'd forgive you not seven,
but seventy-seven times.

A weak woman, I was —
loving such an ungrateful man.

"Angel," you would call me.
And with the voice of the devil himself,
I fell victim to your will.
I was to be faithful to you,
I was to serve you,
I was to sing of your glory,
echoing my devotion for you,
from the heavens to the earth.

And should I even question your
intentions for me,
I would be cursed.

Sounds a lot like religion.

Over you? Right.
If that's what you call
spitting out, uncontrollably, all these lines...
all these clever rhymes.
Wasting all this precious time.

I do it all because *I just like to write.*
I especially love the carpal tunnel,
the way after hours, my eyes begin
to cross, the lines begin to blur,
and my thoughts all slosh and slur.

I just like to type.

The sound of the keyboard clicking
is music to my ears, really.
Who cares that you're no longer here?

All of this effort, it's elective.
I could quit right now, in fact.
Stop writing of you, just like that.

But I can't, you see...
cause *I just like to write.*
And you brought that side out of me.

I missed you before I ever even knew you.
It felt like a homesickness —
a longing for a person I had yet to meet.

Our divorce was hard,
it was *ugly*.
But that's the price you pay, right?
For being young, in love, and naïve?

I thought I had forever with you.
Thought it was all part of the plan.
Thought we'd outgrow our childish
natures, settle our disputes, and grow old,
hand in hand.

I wanted movie nights with our kids,
bedtimes, bath times, and story times.
I wanted it all, for the remainder of our lifetime.
I just wanted you. *Us*. Our family.

So, I'm sorry at the end of it all, you saw another
side of me.
Witnessing that side,
I'm sure I looked bitter, and I looked mean.
But truth is, I was so desperately hurting.

Ever wonder how many poets
immortalized someone unworthy,
into sonnets and alliterations?

How I bet they now roll over in
their graves, dying yet another death,
as they wish to burn those collections
and pages.

I spent years loving the wrong man.
Eating crumbs out of the palm of his hand.
Years, starving.
The yearning kept me
ever searching.
Stomach, always hurting.
A ruthless hunger; a violent churning.
Years, I held my palms out to him,
and pulled my plate away from others
promising to feed me.
As my rib cage shrank,
my self hatred grew.
As my self hatred grew,
I couldn't help but notice,
his ego did too.
But never his love.
And that,
to the young women traveling behind me,
is what I am trying to teach you.
Don't let their presence distort your view.
Don't you dare hand over to them the most
beautiful parts of you.
Hunger for what is real.
Hold your plate out, only for what is true.

Look at you,
so effortlessly living on as the muse,
leaving me, the tortured poet.

You win, I guess. I lose.

Last night I reread all of our old texts,
until I no longer felt a knot in my throat
or a pang in my heart.

Over and over again, I read, until your words
felt more like mere words than the undying love
you once promised it was.

I stared at our photos until I was able to
reduce the image of you in my mind,
to the stranger you have always been.
Not the other half of my soul that I once
believed you to be.

There is no longer an us.
There never was.
Just a you, and a me, existing *separately*.

You weren't a waste of time.
You were worth every poem written,
every royalty earned, every penny and dime —
I mean,
every line,
every rhyme.
My every breath of life.

Now what am I supposed to do?
I spent years keeping you at arms length —
allowing you to draw me in,
only for me to push you away.

You called it inconsistency.
I called it practicing safety.

Cause I'll be goddamned if I ever
allow something so suspicious to
penetrate me; something constructed
so cleverly; *so perfectly.*

Ah, but there you go again,
outsmarting me.
Sliding into me, deeply, dangerously.

You brought a sword to what should
have been a verbal exchange.
I'm wounded now.
(An open gnash, with traces of your DNA.)

And now that you're inside of me,
I fear there is no more pushing you away.

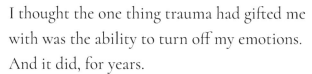

I thought the one thing trauma had gifted me
with was the ability to turn off my emotions.
And it did, for years.
Then, in steps you. *My worst fear.*
Chaotic commotion.
I don't know how or why I didn't see it coming,
with charm, wit, and beauty, as vast as the ocean.

What a fool, to carry such false notion.

The cruelest joke you ever played on me?
Watching you look into her eyes the way
I used to pray you would look into mine.

Let go.
Yeah, I mean, it's just a memory.
It's not like you were as significant as a cell,
or a strand of DNA;
not like you had become a part of me.
Yeah, *I'll let go.*
Of everything that I have ever known.
Of the fairytale Disney taught me.
Of the love the ancient scripts speak of.
Of the reason for this crazy, stupid, delusional
heart inside my chest, beating wildly.
I'll let go.
It's not like what we had, had meaning.
It's a weight off my chest, really.
I'll save on paper, and I'll definitely save on ink.
And I can only imagine the preservation and even the
restoration of what is left of my sanity.
I'll let go.
Our story was juvenile and stupid.
It was embarrassing, really.
In fact, I feel like a child, for ever even believing.
So, *I'll let go.*
Rewiring my brain – what a simple task.
How unbelievably easy.
Yeah, *I'll let go.*
I mean you're the other half of my soul...
but it's not like I need that part of me.

I can't drink away the taste of metallic
as I watch you bleed from afar.
Your heart splits wide open, spews from miles away,
and somehow, for some fucked up reason,
I too must wear your scar.

I'll never forget the moment of your final touch.
Your last finger lifted.
Suddenly the beating of my heart slowed,
my breathing was constricted,
and my entire genetic code had shifted.

I was forever altered by the absence of your skin.
But unfortunately, not enough to forget that we
once existed. Your body, nowhere to be seen,
but I still felt you deep inside of me.

You were roaming the hallways of my mind,
like I was still your home.
You'd mock me, stating I wanted you there,
so why would you leave?
You continued to take up residence, rent free.

How I hated losing you,
only to learn, I in turn, was losing *me*.

A rebel child turned soft soul,
leaving you with a gaping hole
for your backbone to fall through.
Your sorrow for your enemies grew,
as your love for yourself evaded you.

Notice the void,
as your trembling hands pull empathy
out, handing it to those unworthy.
Now stuff yourself back,
and sew yourself shut.
But make sure you stuff
yourself with the highest quality of apathy.

After all, you deserve that.
From the very mouth of your enemies.
(*The ones you try to fix. The ones that laugh as you bleed*).
You hear those words, believe and you receive.

All the while, the world awaits you
to love yourself enough to "rebel" again.

Small talk scares me.
Fear sinks its teeth in like a flesh eating disease.

So your lucky number is five,
and your favorite color is Juniper green.
But in the totality of life,
what does any of that even mean?

You smile as you express your individualism,
and the further I feel you sink.

So tell me...
five, because that's the number of times your dad struck
leather to your bare skin, before letting you free?
Juniper green, because your favorite hiding place
was under your neighbor's backyard tree?

How scared were you, losing your innocence,
at the young age of thirteen?
What age were you when you witnessed the domestic
violence and the drunken stupor screams?

I hope you soon learn, I long to know you
and unravel you. I long to dive your deep.

Nothing is off the table
when it comes to my attempts
at washing your memory away.
Drowning myself in alcohol,
losing myself in lyrics,
lusting after strangers I meet on the subway.

But with a face so goddamn
remarkable, and a voice so painfully
memorable, I see and hear you
inside my mind, mocking,
"I'm here to stay."

Suddenly I find myself
purposely sticking you on a loop,
and you're right back to being my
favorite replay.

Why was I trying to forget you anyway?

Maybe I was old enough.
Twenty-five.
I should heave realized
your intentions after witnessing
your kill-shot gaze, piercing into my eyes.
Should have known better.
Old enough to recognize
that what you had for me wasn't love,
and what I had for you was just a silly,
delusional, school-girl crush.

And it did, it crushed me.

Your words are pretty.
They dance right off the tip of your tongue,
spinning circles around my mind.
They're compelling distractions.
They're potent spells.
But they're anything but truth.

You want me in an altered state?
High, without pharmaceuticals?
To set the tone —
the questions in this poem are going
to be rhetorical.
You want to see me, head so far in the clouds?
Voices screaming your name so loud
I can't drown them out?
You want to see me face down,
dry heaving; fiending,
because it's been days since you've
acknowledged me?
You want to see me hanging on just by a thread?
Screaming into my pillow, because once again,
you've left me on read?
Having panic attacks,
while lighting up palo santo?
You want to move on,
while watching me fail to let go?
You want to leave my body, ice cold,
while lighting a fire inside of my soul?

You want me to want you, yet you don't want me.
That's your end goal.

There are angels disguised as devils,
and devils disguised as angels.
How will we ever know full truth? What is absolute?

And in case you're wondering, *no*.
I do not love you.

I can't lie to you,
and pretend that I have the purest intentions.
I don't.
Pure intentions would be to let you roam free.
I'm too selfish, *I won't.*
There's a possessiveness inside of me.
I want you far too selfishly.
It's a hunger I can't stifle.
An itch I must scratch.
And I would do you a favor and lie to you,
but I think you and I both know,
we're way past that.

I hate the way you say my name.
The rasp in your voice.
The way you shift pace
when you speak to someone else,
then slow down, when you're
speaking to me.
I hate the way your eyes are filled
with a hunger, when you're listening
to me speak.
As if what I'm saying is knowledge,
and you're eager to study.
I hate the way your eyes flicker
with fascination.
You ask me, "why?"
"Why are you so afraid to love?"
As if I owe you, or anyone, for that matter,
an explanation.

But, if I must...
It's your overall charming demeanor.
Your stupid, foolish, inclination towards hope.
The fact, after all the shit life has thrown your way,
you're still a dreamer.
Still not enough?
I can be meaner.

It's that when I stop and look at you for too long,
I have the same, outlandish dreams too.
I want to pick myself up, and try again;
stop putting emphasis on the times I tried,
only to fail.
I want to love you. Really love you.
I want to splash every last color over the grayscale
I have been living inside of the last few years.
I want to abandon all hopelessness and doubt.
I want to love you, without fear.

MENTAL HEALTH HOTLINES:

- *National Alliance on Mental Health (NAMI)*
  Helpline: 1-800-950-NAMI, or text "HELPLINE"
  to 62640

- *National Domestic Violence Hotline:* 1-800-799-7233

- *National Suicide Prevention Lifeline:*
  1-800-273-TALK; or just dial 988

- *Self-harm Hotline:*
  1-800-DONT-CUT

- *Family Violence Helpline:*
  1-800-996-6228

- *Rape Abuse and Incest National Network:*
  (800) 656-HOPE/ (800) 810-7440 (TTY)

- *National Council on Alcoholism & Drug Dependency:*
  1-800-622-2255

ABOUT THE AUTHOR:

Melissa M. Combs, also known as, The Enchanted Poetess, is best known for her collection titled, "Love in Other Realms," but, as of this collection, now holds nine titles to her name.

As a student of life, Melissa believes that every waking moment is another blank page to write into. As she journeys, she tells of her stories through the medium of poetry, in hopes of inspiring others, and to give back to the world surrounding her, as best as she can.

She can usually be found with her family, in nature, or reading and writing. A few of her favorite interests include: the victorian era, collecting ornate antiques and furniture, wine tasting, traveling, and yoga.

FOLLOW HER ON SOCIAL MEDIA:

TikTok: @theenchantedpoetess_

Instagram: @theenchantedpoetess

Threads: @theenchantedpoetess

50245705R00069